101
ways to
dump on
your <u>Ex</u>!

101 ways to dump on your Ex!

BY OAKY MILLER

Cartoons by Mel Crawford

Book Design by Tony La Sala

Published by Spectacle Lane Press

1

Always answer the door in a new low-cut dress when he comes to pick up the children.

2

Wear a peek-a-boo blouse and his favorite perfume when you go to court.

3

Let your ex have the dog when it's in heat.

4

Call your ex-wife's new husband and ask him if her social disease has cleared up yet.

5

Keep telling your ex-mate he's getting fat.

6

Make a date with your ex-wife's sister.

7

Call your ex-husband's boss and ask why he allows his employees to date his wife.

Make your former husband his favorite
cherry pie and leave the pits in.

9

If your ex-mate is heavy, tell her
she's a perfect 20....two 10's.

10

For Valentine's Day send your ex
a heart-shaped box of Ex-Lax.

11

Call your ex-wife at 3:00 A.M.
to explain why you'll be
late with your support check.

12

Rent a Mercedes to pick
up the children.

13

Send your ex-mate a
Candygram collect.

14

When you visit your ex-mate, steal
all the toilet paper in the house.

15

Call your ex-wife's favorite depart-
ment store anonymously and ask the
credit manager how many bounced
checks she has written this month.

16

Knowing your ex-wife has allergies, send her new boy friend two free tickets to a hayride.

17

Anonymously send your ex-mate
a bottle of Scope for Christmas.

18

Send a large cheesecake
to your dieting ex.

Put a sign in front of your ex-wife's
house saying: GYPSIES - FORTUNE
TELLING, PRIVATE READINGS.

Next time you're at your former
spouse's, pinprick the water bed.

21

Send a telegram to your ex telling him
to forget the first wire you sent.

22

Call your ex-husband's new wife
and ask her if he still likes to parade
around the house in a brassiere.

23

Tell your ex-mate that the
maitre d' at his favorite restaurant
asked about him again.

24

Never have the children ready when he comes for weekend outings.

25

Call your ex-wife five days in a row and tell her the check is in the mail.

26

Phone the head of the Hell's Angels and call him a fag, then give your former wife's address.

27

Siphon gas out of your ex-husband's new car every week so he'll think it's a gas hog.

23

Never bring the children home
on time. Explain that your
new girlfriend was making fudge
brownies for the kids.

29

Tell your ex-mate that you
saw her new boyfriend's
picture in the post office.

30

Call a telethon and pledge $10,000
in your ex-mate's name.

31

Call your ex and give him
the wrong directions to visit
the kids at summer camp.

32

Tell the neighbors you're collecting for a rummage sale and have them dump the stuff on your ex-mate's front lawn.

33

Substitute Crazy Glue for your
ex-husband's toupee adhesive.

34

Spread the word around your church
that your ex-mate cheats at bingo.

35

Put water from Mexico in Perrier
bottles and leave them on the door
step of your ex-mate's house.

36

Give your ex-husband a "Two-for-one Dinner" book good only at a restaurant that is out of business.

37

Show up in court with your ex-mate's best friend as your attorney.

38

Rubber-stamp your ex-wife's phone number on the walls of men's rooms.

39

If your ex-mate has been trying to lose weight for sometime, ask her when she is planning to start her diet.

Inform your ex-husband it's his turn to bring coffee and doughnuts to the next PTA meeting, but don't tell him it's been cancelled.

41

Buy a chance on a used Pinto in your ex-mate's name.

42

Hire an airplane to fly over your ex-wife's house pulling a banner reading, "You're Getting Old!"

43

Send you former spouse matchbook covers from motels around the world.

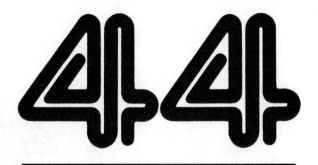

Volunteer your ex-husband to
take the entire Cub Scout pack
to Disneyland as his treat.

45

Send your ex-husband to a dentist that doesn't believe in using novocaine.

46

Call your ex-mate on his answering machine every day and leave an incomplete message.

47

Make sure the children ask their mother why she has to work and Daddy's new girlfriend doesn't.

43

If your ex-husband is bald, send
him a picture of you with a
very hairy guy you are dating.

49

Send your ex a bottle of Grecian Formula on his next birthday.

50

If your ex-wife is flat chested, send her a "D" cup bra with "Ha! Ha!" written on each cup.

51

Knowing your ex-husband couldn't tell the difference, scrape the bottoms off all his Teflon cookware.

52

Call up your ex-husband's
new wife and ask her if he still
wants to do it six times a night.

53

Re-label your ex-husband's shaving cream with a whipped cream label.

54

Park in front of your ex-mate's apartment with your new love interest and make out.

55

If your wife has varicose veins, ask her when she started wearing fishnet stockings.

56

Call your ex-husband and ask if he wants
to buy his old bed because you and
your boy friend are picking out a new one.

57

Call your ex-mate twenty times on
his answering machine and hang up.

58

Spread the word that your
ex-wife wears falsies.

59

Put Saran Wrap inside
the lids of your ex-husband's
salt and pepper shakers.

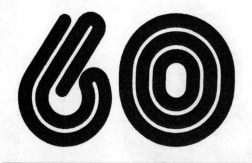

Carve your ex-husband's
new girl friend's initials on
his prized new sports car.

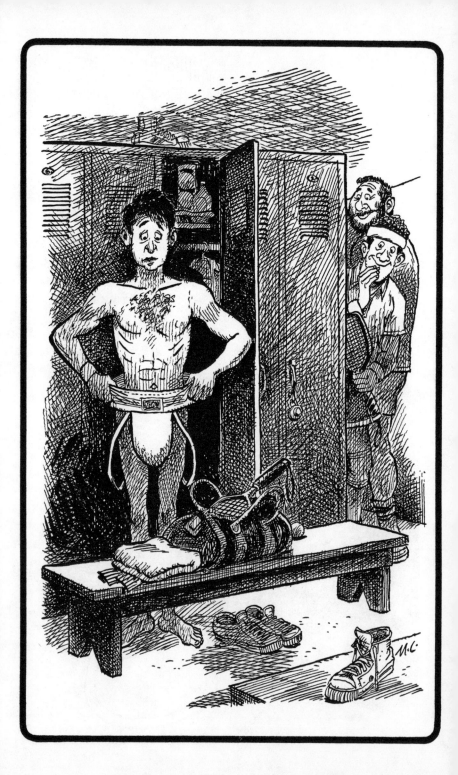

61

Order a termite fumigation
for your ex-mate's new house.

62

Replace your ex-husband's regular
athletic supporter in his
gym bag with a king-sized one.

63

When a magazine salesman comes
to your door, order everything he has
and send the bill to your ex-mate.

64

Introduce a box of mites to
your ex-wife's prize roses.

65

Put lavender dye in your
ex-husband's laundry detergent.

66

Pour an oil spot under your
ex-husband's new car once a week.

67

When it's your ex-husband's
visitation weekend, make sure your
children each bring three friends along.

68

Ask your ex-husband's landlady why she allows immoral acts on her property.

69

Send your former spouse a rotten horoscope for her birthday.

70

Order excavation to begin on a swimming pool in your ex-mate's front yard.

71

Tell the Rose Bowl Committee that they can have all the flowers at your ex-wife's house.

72

Substitute fertility pills for your ex-wife's birth control pills.

73

Call your ex-wife "Crisco" because she is fat in the can.

74

Put a "Have You Paid Your Child Support Today?" sticker on your ex-husband's car bumper.

75

When you meet your ex-husband's boss, ask him why your ex-husband always said his boss was fat.

76

Call your ex-wife's new husband
and ask if she still likes to see
her old girlfriend she calls Butch.

77

Tell Goodwill to pick up all the
lawn furniture on your ex-wife's lawn.

78

For his birthday send your ex-husband
swimming trunks two sizes to small.

79

Knowing that your ex-wife listens
to sex counselor Dr. Ruth on the radio,
call up and tell Dr. Ruth how happy
you are with your new lover.

If your ex-husband travels a lot, secretly sew metal strips into his pants lining, so he will keep setting off the airport alarm.

81

Ask the children not to tell their friends that your ex-wife puts left-overs in her pies.

82

Put nicks in the shaving head of your ex-husband's electric razor.

83

The next time you see your ex-mate at a family gathering, tell him in a loud voice that you're glad to see he's sober for once.

84

Send notes to all the male employees where your ex-wife works saying she moonlights in a massage parlor.

85

Cancel all your ex-husband's season tickets for his favorite team's games.

86

When your ex-wife goes away on her dream vacation give her a dozen rolls of pre-exposed film.

87

Adjust the sprinkler heads on your ex-mate's lawn to create a permanent display of dancing waters.

If your ex-wife is flat-chested,
send her a picture of Dolly Parton.

89

Let the children play
postman with your ex-husband's
rare stamp collection.

90

Spread the word that your ex-wife is
deaf, even though she hears perfectly.

91

Spread the word among the neighborhood
children that your ex-wife pays
top dollar for recycled aluminum cans.

92

Knowing that your ex is an avid camper, put itching powder in his sleeping bag.

93

Put a couple of loose screws in the
hubcaps of your ex-mate's new car.

94

Knowing your ex-wife is deathly
afraid of rodents, give the children
a pair of pet mice for Christmas.

95

Call the city and tell them
to prune all the trees in front
of your ex-wife's new house.

Inform the vice squad that your ex-mate
is growing things other than vegetables.

97

For protection, make sure your
ex-wife gets an empty can of Mace.

98

When your ex-husband
goes on vacation, pull the
plug on his freezer.

99

Knowing your ex-husband likes
to sleep late on weekends, make
sure the children always call
him early in the morning.

Substitute Crazy Glue for
your ex-husband's Polident.

101

When your youngest child turns 18
and there is no more child support,
throw a party and show your
ex-wife how high you're living.

Published by Spectacle Lane Press